Sea Horses

Sea Horses

by Sally M. Walker
A Carolrhoda Nature Watch Book

Enjoy learning about these neat
little fish. The <u>dads</u> have the babies,
not the moms.
Best wishes,
Sally M. Walker

Carolrhoda Books, Inc. / Minneapolis

*For the people of Handumon village in the
Philippines, with admiration. Thinking of
the future, they have made changes that
benefit sea horses, other fishes, and people.*

*The author thanks Dr. Amanda Vincent for graciously sharing
her time and knowledge. Her studies of sea horses in the
laboratory and in the wild, plus her commitment to focusing
worldwide attention on sea horses and the need for their
conservation, prove that one person really can make a difference.
Thanks also to Kurt Stephenson at the John G. Shedd Aquarium
for the behind-the-scenes sea horse tour.*

Text copyright © 1999 by Sally M. Walker

Carolrhoda Books, Inc., c/o The Lerner Publishing Group
241 First Avenue North, Minneapolis, MN 55401 U.S.A.

Website address: www.lernerbooks.com

LIBRARY OF CONGRESS CATALOGING-IN-PUBLICATION DATA

Walker, Sally M.
 Sea horses / by Sally M. Walker.
  p. cm.
 "A Carolrhoda nature watch book."
 Includes index.
 Summary: Describes the physical characteristics, life
cycle, and behavior of sea horses as well as efforts to
protect them.
  ISBN 1-57505-317-9
  1. Sea horses—Juvenile literature. [1. Sea horses.]
I. Title.
QL638.S9W35 1999
597'.6798—DC21   98-14440

Manufactured in the United States of America
1 2 3 4 5 6 – JR – 04 03 02 01 00 99

CONTENTS

A MOST UNUSUAL FISH

As a water current ripples through a coral reef, a small head peers around one of the branches. The head is shaped much like a horse's head, but the rest of the creature doesn't look at all like a horse. Prickly looking skin covers its body. The creature's long tail wraps firmly around the branch of coral, grasping it the way a monkey's tail grasps a tree branch.

An artist's vision of a
mythological sea horse,
drawn in the year 1536

This unusual fish, the sea horse, has fascinated people for thousands of years. In ancient Greek mythology, Poseidon, the god of the sea, drove a chariot pulled by a giant sea horse. Some myths tell about gods riding the waves on the backs of huge sea horses. In ancient art, sea horses are often shown with heads and front legs that look exactly like those of land-dwelling horses. And for hundreds of years, people have used sea horses as an ingredient in medicines, hoping to cure conditions ranging from baldness to poor appetite to heart disease.

The most interesting thing about sea horses has nothing to do with mythology or medicine. It has to do with sea horses themselves. Female sea horses do not give birth to babies—males do! And that's just one of the many reasons they're such amazing fish. Unfortunately, each year millions of sea horses are caught and removed from Earth's oceans. If this trend continues, sea horses will become **endangered,** or at risk of dying out forever.

Scientists classify, or arrange, animals into groups according to their characteristics. Sea horses and other types of fish that have skeletons made of bones belong to a class, or large scientific grouping, called Osteichthyes (ah-stee-ICK-thees). The word *osteichthyes* comes from two Latin words that mean "bony fishes." Bony fishes first appeared on Earth about 410 million years ago. Over time, they have evolved, or changed, into many different types of fish. Scientists believe sea horses evolved at least 40 million years ago.

Along with the sea horse, the class Osteichthyes includes fishes such as the moray eel (above left), *the African lungfish* (top right), *and the smallmouth bass* (bottom right).

Sea horses belong to a family, or smaller grouping, that scientists have named the Syngnathidae (sing-NATH-ih-dee). Sea dragons, pipefish, and pipehorses are also syngnathids, or members of the Syngnathidae family. These fishes all have tube-shaped snouts with small mouths. Male syngnathids take care of the eggs until they hatch.

Top right: *A sea horse meets face-to-face with one of its cousins, a long, skinny pipefish.*
Below: *The leafy sea dragon is another relative of the sea horse.*

A sea dragon's eggs are embedded on the male's tail (above) until they are ready to hatch.

9

Scientists classify syngnathids into even smaller groups that are alike in certain ways. Each of these groups is called a genus. Sea horses belong to the genus *Hippocampus.* The word *hippocampus* comes from two Greek words: *hippos,* meaning horse, and *kampos,* meaning sea monster or worm.

Within the genus *Hippocampus,* scientists think there are about 35 different **species,** or kinds, of sea horses. They aren't sure how many species exist because studying sea horses in the wild is difficult. Marine biologists, scientists who study sea life, must spend lots of time underwater, which can be expensive and dangerous. Sea horses have only been studied in the wild since the 1980s.

For this reason, scientists still have many unanswered questions about them.

Unfortunately, the 35 sea horse species that scientists have identified are referred to by about 120 different common names. That means that a single species often has several common names, so talking about sea horses can be confusing.

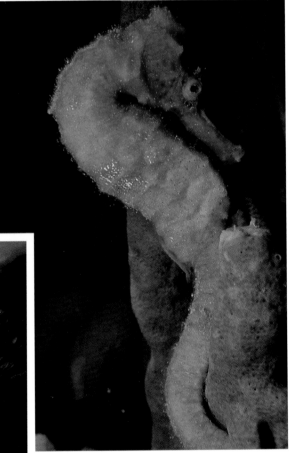

Above: Hippocampus reidi, *one of about 35 sea horse species*
Left: *Studying sea horses is harder than just peeking into an aquarium.*

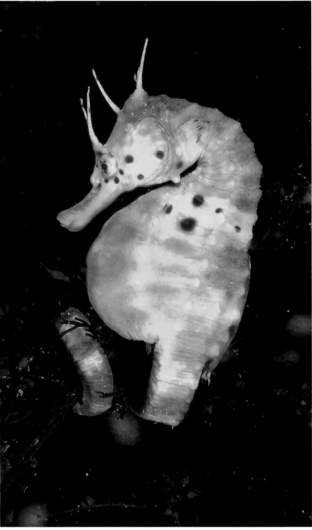

Scientists hope to sort out the confusion over common names by studying sea horse **genes,** tiny structures in the cells of living things that are passed from parents to their young. Genes determine characteristics such as size and color. Each sea horse species has its own unique pattern of genes. Learning about sea horse genes will help scientists narrow down the number of common names for sea horses.

Until this research is complete, scientists have agreed to call sea horses by their scientific names, which include genus and species. Since the genus name *Hippocampus* is long, it's abbreviated as *H.* So, for example, *H. abdominalis* is the scientific name for one species of sea horse that has a particularly large abdomen, or belly.

11

Sea horses live in three main **habitats,** or kinds of environments. Sea grass beds are thick patches of aquatic, or water-dwelling, plants. They look like underwater meadows. Sea horses like to live along the edges of sea grass beds, where water from the open sea flows freely. This oxygen-rich water attracts other animals to the area, creating a plentiful food source for sea horses.

Sea horses also live among stands, or groups, of mangroves, tropical trees that grow along the coastline in shallow ocean waters. Coral reefs, the sea horse's third habitat, are ridges found on the ocean floor in warm, shallow waters. Coral reefs are made of the skeletons of many tiny sea animals.

Blades of sea grass, tangled mangrove roots, and branchlike corals make handy **holdfasts,** objects a sea horse can grasp with its long, curled tail. Thick plant growth and ridged corals also help sea horses hide from animals that could catch and eat them. All three habitats teem with small animals that sea horses like to eat.

Top: *A thick sea grass bed*
Middle: *An underwater view of a stand of mangroves*
Bottom: *A coral reef in the Caribbean Sea*

12

Sea horses usually live in salt water that ranges from about 3 to 50 feet deep (1–15 m). Most species live in fairly warm water and can tolerate temperatures up to about 86°F (30°C). They do not usually live in water that gets colder than about 43°F (6°C).

Eleven of the world's sea horse species live in warm ocean waters near Australia. Four species are found in North American and South American waters, and two species live in European coastal waters. The rest of the world's sea horse species live in the Indian Ocean and in the western Pacific Ocean, ranging as far north as the Korean Peninsula.

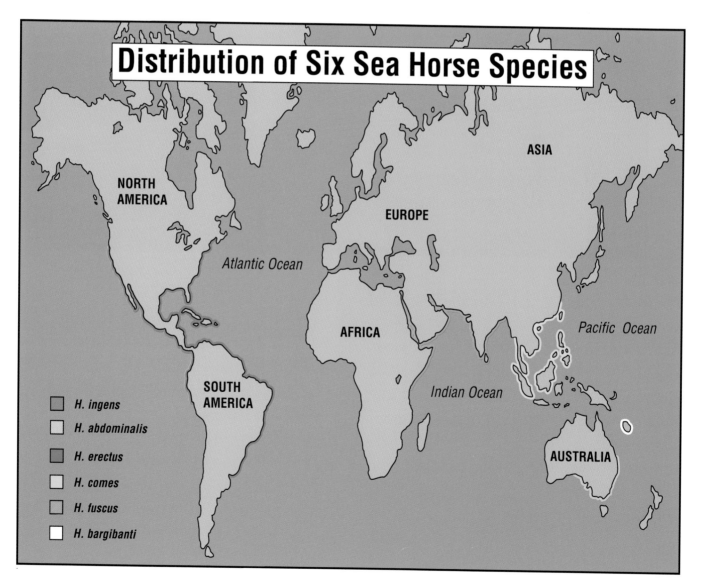

Distribution of Six Sea Horse Species

NORTH AMERICA

ASIA

EUROPE

Atlantic Ocean

AFRICA

Pacific Ocean

SOUTH AMERICA

Indian Ocean

AUSTRALIA

- ☐ *H. ingens*
- ☐ *H. abdominalis*
- ☐ *H. erectus*
- ☐ *H. comes*
- ☐ *H. fuscus*
- ☐ *H. bargibanti*

Length* Comparison of Six Sea Horse Species

H. ingens
14 inches (35 cm)

H. abdominalis
10 inches (25 cm)

H. comes
7 inches (18 cm)

H. erectus
7 inches (18 cm)

H. fuscus
3.5 inches (9 cm)

H. bargibanti
0.5 inches
(1.3 cm)

INCHES

15

10

5

0

*Measurements are from end of snout to tip of tail.

PHYSICAL CHARACTERISTICS

Sea horse species range in size from tiny *H. bargibanti*, which is less than an inch long, up to *H. ingens*, the largest species, which may be 14 inches long (35 cm). In most animal species, the males tend to be larger than the females. But male and female sea horses of most species are about the same size as one another.

Sea horse skeletons are different from those of other bony fishes. In addition to a backbone, which all bony fishes have, sea horses have a series of knobby, bony plates arranged in rings. The rings extend down the **trunk,** or the main part of the body, becoming smaller and more numerous toward the tip of the tail. The number of rings a sea horse has varies from species to species—*H. trimaculatus* has 41 rings on its tail alone.

The many bony rings make a sea horse's tail very flexible, or easy to bend. Like monkeys and opossums, which live on land, sea horses have **prehensile** tails that can wrap around and grasp objects. Sea horses are poor swimmers, and they must constantly fight flowing water currents that could sweep them away. So it's helpful to have tails that can hold their bodies in place. A sea horse will wrap its tail around any object it finds, including the finger of a person who picks it up.

Sea horses do not have scales. Instead, the bony rings are covered only by skin. The skin stretches tightly across the rings, like your skin stretches over your knuckles when you make a fist. This gives the sea horse its ridged appearance. Sea horse skin is very tough. When scientists have to give a sick sea horse an injection, it may take a few tries to get the needle to poke through the skin.

Top: *This colored X ray shows the bony rings that start at a sea horse's head and extend all the way down its trunk to the tail.*
Right: *The tightly curled tail of an* H. kuda

Fish breathe by passing water over organs called gills. Oxygen passes from the water into blood vessels on the gills. The blood vessels carry the oxygen throughout the fish's body. Most fishes have several comblike rows of gills on each side of the head, but sea horse gills aren't in rows. They're clustered in clumps, like bunches of grapes.

Another difference between sea horses and other bony fishes is the way they swim. Most fishes use strong tail fins to push themselves headfirst through the water. Sea horses swim upright, with their tails pointing downward. Swimming upright helps the sea horse to turn quickly and squeeze between plant blades or mangrove roots. When a sea horse wants to swim at its fastest speed, it tilts forward, into a horizontal position.

If a trout or shark tried to swim upright, its eyes would face upward and it wouldn't be able to see where it was going. Sea horses can swim upright—and see where they are going—because unlike other fishes, they have necks. The neck allows a sea horse's head to bend, so the sea horse can look forward no matter what position it is in.

Because it has a neck, this H. ingens *can see straight ahead whether it's upright or horizontal.*

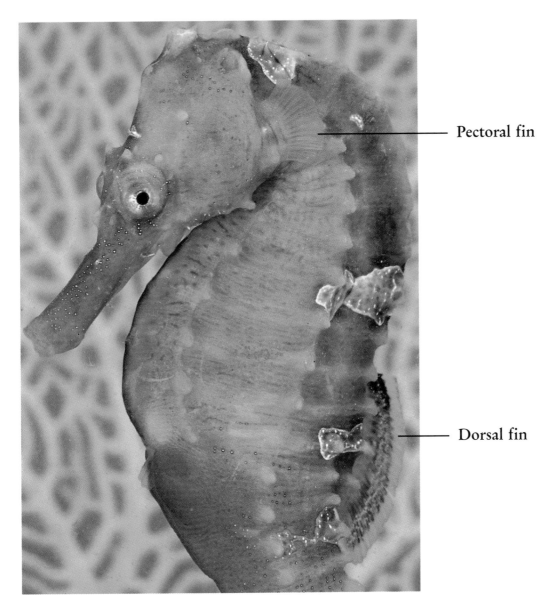

Pectoral fin

Dorsal fin

Like other bony fishes, sea horses have a dorsal fin, a fin on the back. A sea horse's dorsal fin ripples back and forth 35 to 41 times per second—too fast for a human to see the individual waves. If a sea horse does not wave its dorsal fin, its body sinks.

A sea horse also has a small pectoral fin on each side of its head, near where you might expect to see ears. The pectoral fins are used for steering and steadying the sea horse's body. Thanks to their fins, sea horses can twist and turn easily and even swim in a spiral pattern.

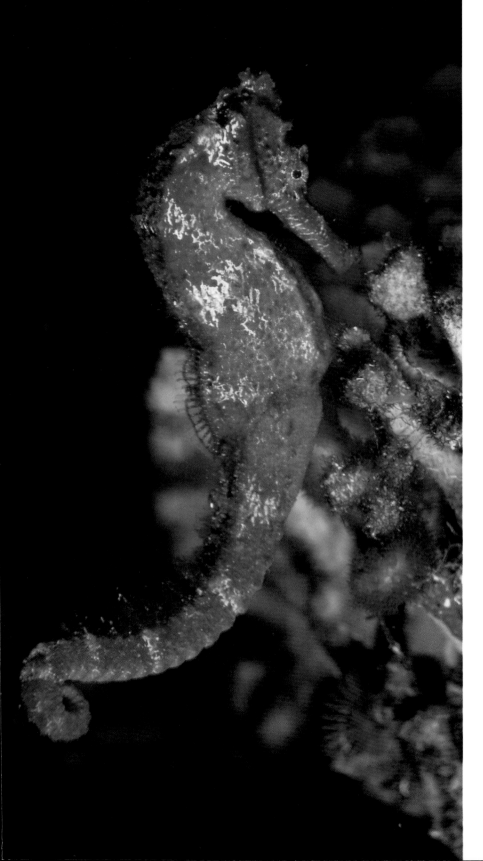

This H. reidi *can use its swim bladder to rise, sink, or hover in the water.*

Like many fishes, every sea horse has a **swim bladder** that helps it move up and down in the water. A swim bladder is a bit like a small balloon or air bag. It contains gases such as oxygen and nitrogen. These gases are passed from the sea horse's gills into its blood when the sea horse breathes. When a sea horse wants to move upward, it lets gas from its bloodstream fill the swim bladder. The air-filled bladder makes the sea horse rise, the same way an air-filled balloon would rise if you pushed it down into water and then let it go. When a sea horse wants to sink again, it can force gas from the swim bladder back into its bloodstream.

19

Above: *A whitetip reef shark cruises through Hawaiian waters.*
Left: *A blue-spotted stingray hunts over a coral reef.*

PREDATORS AND PREY

Sea horses are **predators,** animals that eat other animals. They are also **prey,** animals that other animals eat. Crabs, skates, rays, and sharks prey on sea horses. Baby sea horses are frequently snapped up by other fishes, too. Marine biologists have also seen penguins and other seabirds eat sea horses.

Sea horses try to avoid these predators in several ways. They are very good at staying completely still. Their long, upright bodies help them hide among plants. Sea horses can also blend in with their surroundings in an even trickier way. They can **camouflage** (KAM-uh-flahzh), or disguise, themselves by changing their color and appearance.

Normally, most sea horse species range in color from tan to brown to black. They may also have spots or stripes. When a sea horse holds on to a piece of brightly colored coral, it often changes color to match. It isn't unusual to find sea horses in different shades of red, yellow, orange, or even green. Even the iris, or outer rim, of a sea horse's eye can change color.

Another way a sea horse uses camouflage is by growing **tendrils,** stringlike stems of skin, on its head and back. Small creatures cluster about the tendrils, and bits of plants often get caught on them. Tiny animals will also settle onto a sea horse's body. As they accumulate and grow, they make the sea horse look crusty. Together, these kinds of camouflage make spotting a sea horse quite difficult.

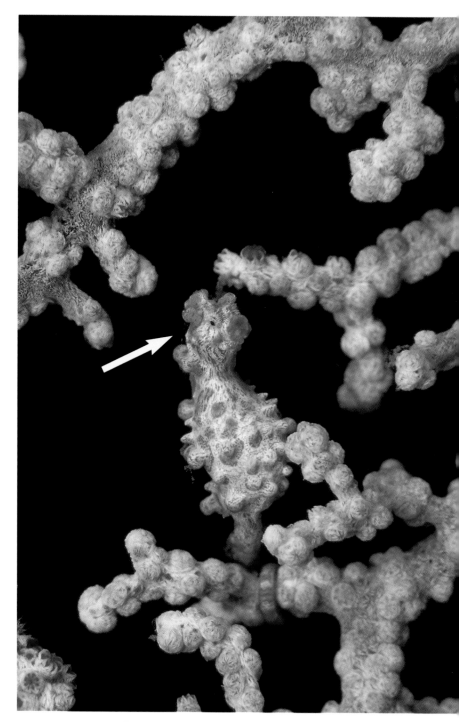

Can you spot the tiny, well-camouflaged H. bargibanti *hiding in this bumpy coral reef? (The arrow is pointing to its head.)*

Sea horses are also able to keep a sharp lookout for predators. Sea horses can move their eyes in separate directions. One eye can look upward while the other looks down. Marine biologists believe that sea horses can see colors and that they have sharp vision, particularly in the daytime. That's important, because when they get hungry, they must be able to zero in on tiny prey.

Sea horses spend most of their time eating. They eat tiny shrimp and other crustaceans, animals that have a hard outer shell and usually live in water. Some of the crustaceans sea horses eat are so tiny that about three million of them would fit in a single bathtub filled with water. Sea horses also like to eat the **larvae,** or early growth stages, of fishes and sponges.

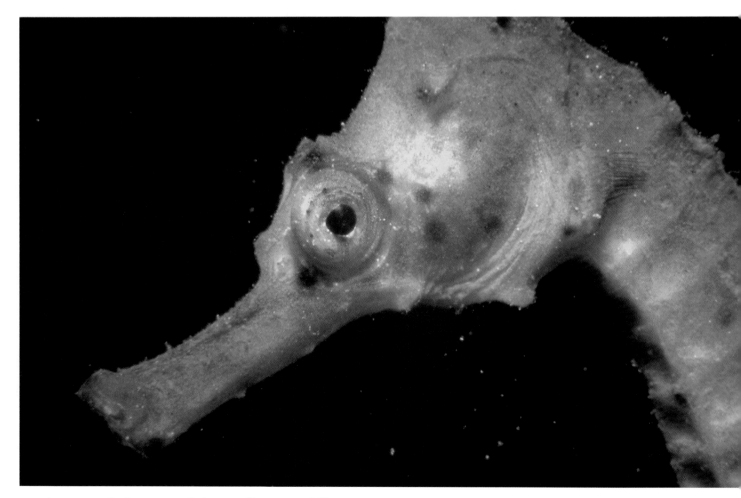

A close-up of the powerful eye of an H. reidi

Above: *These crustacean larvae have been magnified many times.*
Right: *An* H. ingens *hunts for a meal.*

To hunt, a sea horse clings to its hold-fast, almost motionless, until prey swims by. Its eyes zero in on the target. Suddenly, the sea horse's head darts forward. Its lower lip drops open, and the sea horse quickly sucks the prey into its long, tube-shaped snout. It takes only 6 milliseconds for a sea horse to suck in a tiny crustacean—that's faster than the blink of an eye. After the prey has been captured, the sea horse's lower lip flips up and covers the end of its snout, almost like a lid.

A sea horse has no teeth, so it just swallows its food whole. But the food doesn't go into a stomach, because a sea horse has no stomach either! Instead, food passes to the intestines, where it is broken down and absorbed by the sea horse's body. Whatever remains at the end of the process is passed out as **feces,** or solid waste matter.

Marine biologists don't know whether sea horses can taste or smell their prey. They also don't know how well sea horses hear. They do know that sea horses can make a clicking noise. Sea horses have a small, V-shaped protrusion on the underside of the snout. When the mouth opens, the protrusion flicks downward and clicks. Sea horses make these clicks, which can be loud or soft, while they are eating. Biologists are trying to find out if sea horses use the clicks to communicate.

The snout of this H. abdominalis *is not only a vacuum cleaner for sucking in food—it can also make noise.*

Unless they live in an aquarium, sea horse couples are rarely seen together.

SOCIAL LIFE AND DAILY GREETINGS

Many types of fish live in schools, or large groups. Sea horses do not. Sometimes two pairs of sea horses are seen together. At night, *H. abdominalis* may cluster in mixed groups of males and females. Most of the time, however, sea horses are alone.

Dr. Amanda Vincent, a marine biologist, was the first scientist to study sea horses underwater in the wild. While observing *H. whitei* near Sydney, Australia, she found that each sea horse has a **home range,** or an area where it lives, roams, and produces young. The size of a sea horse's home range varies according to its species and sex. The home range of a male *H. whitei* is about 11 square feet (1 sq m), close to the size of a card table. Within his home range, a male may stay anchored to the same blade of sea grass for several days. Female *H. whitei* range over a wider area—about 1,075 square feet (100 sq m), almost half the size of a tennis court. A female's home range overlaps several male home ranges.

25

Two H. ingens engage in a wrestling match.

Many animals have a **breeding season,** or a specific time of year when they produce young. Some sea horses have a breeding season, but others don't. The breeding season for *H. whitei* is about 7 months long. In contrast, *H. comes,* a species that lives in the Philippines, breeds all year long.

When it is time to breed, any fully grown sea horse without a mate will seek one. In the wild, males rarely have to compete for a mate. Most sea horse populations are spread out so that male home ranges don't overlap much, and competition isn't necessary. If, however, storms or fishing nets have killed many sea horses, the remaining males may have to compete for the reduced number of females. In laboratory aquariums, where sea horses are kept close together, males do compete for a mate.

Males compete for a female in several ways. One male may grasp the other with his tail, resulting in a bout of tail wrestling. Flattening, or pushing a rival against the bottom of the tank or ocean floor, is another competitive behavior. A male sea horse may also snap at his rival by flicking his snout quickly toward the rival's gills and pectoral fins. Some snaps are hard enough to shove a rival as far as 4 inches (10 cm).

Biologists don't know for sure how a female chooses the male with which she will bond, or form a partnership. They believe her first choice may be a male that is about the same length that she is. Once a female and male bond, they remain completely faithful to each other for at least that breeding season, and possibly longer. (Biologists are still studying how long pair bonds last.) The female acknowledges only her mate. When she passes through another male's home range, she ignores him.

A sea horse will choose a new mate only if its first mate dies or disappears. If a sea horse must choose a new mate, however, it won't be picky. It will bond with the first available sea horse it meets.

At least one species of sea horse studied so far—H. abdominalis—*is different from the others. H.* abdominalis *may not maintain loyal pair bonds, as other sea horse species do. Instead of clinging constantly to a holdfast, it curls up in sandy hollows on the ocean floor. The species is also set apart by its huge, lumpy belly and by the size of the males, which are larger than the females. Marine biologists are trying to find out why this species is so unusual and whether others might have similar behaviors.*

Daily greetings, or regular morning meetings, are an important part of sea horse pair bonding. Every morning, shortly after first light, the female swims into the male's home range and visits for 6 to 10 minutes. First, the male and female swim to their usual greeting place. They **brighten,** or quickly change to a brighter color than normal. For example, *H. fuscus* is normally black. When it brightens, its color ranges from creamy pink to yellow.

After brightening, the mates wrap their tails around the same holdfast and swim around it, like circling a maypole. Occasionally, they let go of the holdfast and swim a short distance across the bottom, tails linked. They alternate between circling and swimming together until one of them darkens and does not respond to the other's motions. Then the daily greeting ends, and the female swims away. The next day, she will return to greet her mate again.

LIFE CYCLE

The smaller species of sea horses are ready to mate at about 3 months old. Larger species start mating when they are between 6 months and a year old. By this time, a female sea horse has developed an **ovipositor,** a tube that can extend outside her body to lay eggs. A male sea horse has a **brood pouch,** or pocket that protects and nurtures eggs, on his tail.

A sea horse's brood pouch is a fascinating place. Many animal mothers, such as kangaroos, koalas, and opossums, have pouches in which their newborn young spend their early days. A sea horse's pouch is unique because it is found on the father's body—and because the young grow inside it before they are born.

Before mating takes place, the lining on the inside of the pouch thickens and becomes spongelike in preparation for receiving eggs. The number of blood vessels in the pouch's lining increases. These blood vessels will carry oxygen to the growing babies and remove waste material from inside the eggs.

Can you spot the brood pouch opening of this pregnant male H. breviceps?

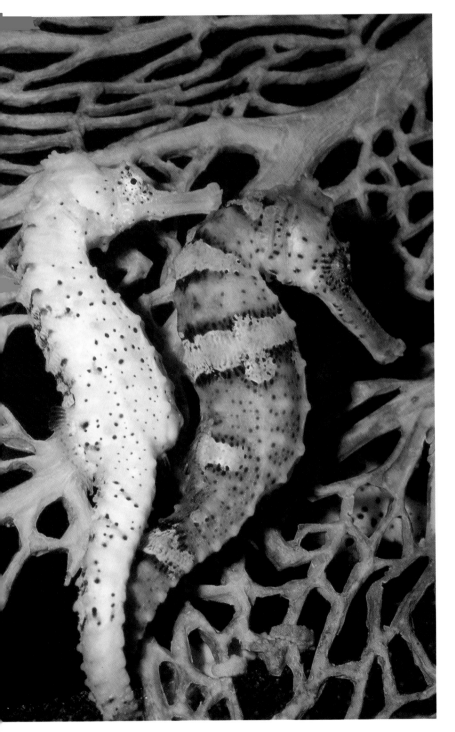

The courtship dance has begun for these mates.

When sea horses are ready to mate, they begin courtship. Courtship has four stages and may last from several hours up to 3 days. It begins as an extension of the daily greeting, with both sea horses brightened. The sea horses cling to the same holdfast. They quiver and tilt at each other for several minutes.

By the second stage of courtship, the female's belly has grown round from the eggs inside her. It's often possible to see their orange color through her skin. The female begins **pointing.** She raises her head and points her snout toward the surface of the water. The male responds by **pumping,** bending his tail forward and upward. He also opens the hole in the top of his brood pouch. The pumping motion squeezes water in and out of his pouch. Biologists believe the male may do this to signal to the female that his pouch is empty and ready for eggs.

A male (right) *holds open his brood pouch to receive his mate's eggs.*

During the third courtship stage, both sea horses point and brighten many times. In the fourth and last stage, they float upward together several times. When their bellies are lined up, the female places her ovipositor into the hole at the top of the male's pouch. She quickly deposits her eggs. This takes about 6 to 10 seconds for a female *H. whitei.* The male's pouch becomes swollen and full, while the female's body becomes slender again. From this point, the male takes care of the eggs alone.

Inside the pouch, sperm cells from the male combine with the eggs to make them fertile, or able to develop. At this stage, the young sea horses, which are called **embryos,** begin to grow inside the eggs. The male squeezes the muscle around the pouch hole to close it, then sinks to the ocean floor and sways back and forth. This rocking motion settles the eggs. A tissue seal forms behind the hole to give the eggs further protection.

Soon, the broad end of each pear-shaped egg becomes embedded in the pouch wall. Tissue wraps around most of the egg, enclosing it within its own tissue pocket. The narrow end of the egg is not covered by tissue. Biologists believe the embryo receives nourishment from the fluid inside the pouch. This fluid enters the egg through its uncovered end. Any eggs that are not surrounded by tissue will eventually dissolve.

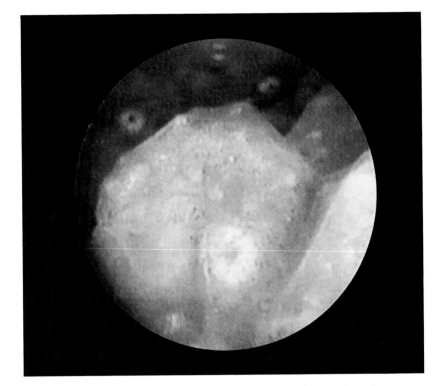

Inside its father's pouch, a sea horse embryo develops within its egg. This photo and those on page 33 were taken with a tiny camera that was inserted into the father's pouch opening. The father and babies were not harmed.

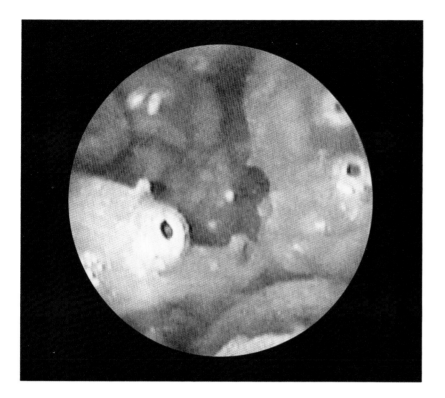

The pouch fluid changes during the pregnancy. The shell of each egg and the thin membrane, or tissue, beneath the shell slowly dissolve, adding nutrients to the pouch fluid. Gradually, the fluid also becomes saltier, like seawater. By the time the babies are born, they are accustomed to a saltwater environment and are ready to leave their father's care.

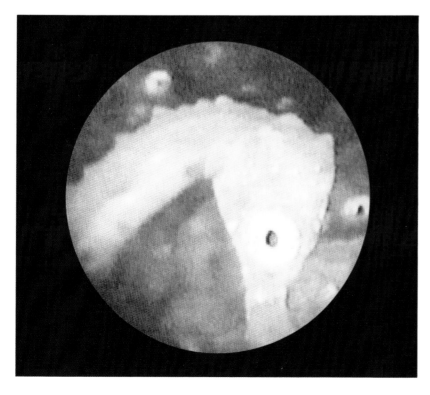

Top: *As the embryos grow, the shells of the eggs slowly dissolve.* Bottom: *Free of its egg, this embryo is almost ready to be born.*

33

The father's pregnancy lasts from 10 days to 6 weeks, depending on the species and conditions in the habitat. Warmer water temperatures will shorten the pregnancy. When the young are ready to be born, the male relaxes the muscle that holds his pouch closed, then begins pumping. This time, water isn't forced out. Instead, bursts of tiny sea horses are!

It usually takes a few hours to deliver all the young. As soon as the male finishes giving birth, he is ready to become pregnant again. The female has visited her mate for daily greetings throughout his pregnancy, so she knows this. They will usually mate again within a day.

A male sea horse gives birth.

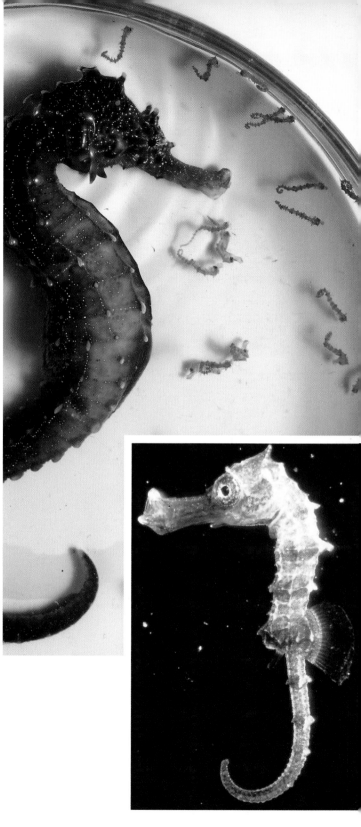

Right: *An* H. kuda *father and babies in a laboratory*
Bottom: *Close-up of a newborn* H. reidi

Brood size, or the number of young born, varies with species and size. Tiny *H. zosterae* gives birth to about a dozen young. The males of larger species give birth to 100 to 200 young. The largest known brood size belonged to an *H. reidi* that gave birth to 1,572 babies! During a successful breeding season, a pair of medium-sized sea horses will produce about 1,000 babies. An average of only 2 will survive to adulthood.

Newborn sea horses are about 0.3 to 0.5 inches long (7–12 mm). That's roughly the length of your little fingernail from base to tip. The baby sea horses in a medium-sized sea horse's brood pouch would fill about half a tablespoon. If they were straightened and placed end to end, the line would be about 36 feet long (11 m)!

Baby sea horses have some color, but they are slightly transparent. Their gills can be seen through their bodies. Gradually, the skin darkens to the normal color of the sea horse's species.

Young sea horses are fully independent from birth. Neither the father nor the mother plays a further role in raising them. Seconds after being born, the babies sink and try to settle into material on the ocean floor. Their tails grab onto anything that might serve as a holdfast, even another baby sea horse.

Above: *These* H. hudsonius *live in an aquarium. In the wild, young sea horses live independently of their parents from birth.*

Finding a holdfast quickly is important, because the baby must begin to catch food. Baby sea horses are very eager eaters. They eat thousands of crustaceans, larvae, and other tiny animals every day. Catching that much food isn't easy, and many young sea horses starve.

Young sea horses also face many other challenges to their survival. They must avoid fishes that could eat them and currents that could whisk them away into the open sea. Baby sea horses often seek shelter in mats of floating seaweed. The plants provide plenty of holdfasts and attract other baby animals, which make a good food source.

The young that are fortunate enough to survive grow in rapid spurts. They will continue to grow throughout their lives, though their growth rate slows when they become adults. The smaller sea horse species seem to have a life span of about a year. Medium-sized and large species may live 4 years or more. Unfortunately, millions of sea horses won't live that long. They will be captured and killed by humans.

Above and left: *Newborns cling to their first holdfast.*

Setting out to fish for sea horses in the Philippines

SEA HORSES AND PEOPLE

Some sea animals prey on sea horses, but humans pose a much greater threat. Each year, people catch and kill millions of adult sea horses. People remove them faster than the sea horses can mate and produce young. In recent years, sea horses have become more sought after than in the past. It's important to understand why the demand for sea horses has increased, since it will affect the long-term survival of these unique fish.

In some parts of the world, fish is a main part of people's diets. Fishers in countries like the Philippines catch fish both to feed their families and to sell. They use the money to buy rice and other items their families need to survive. Fishers first choose to hunt fishes that people want to eat, because these fishes sell well in markets.

As the human population increases, markets need more fish to sell. Fishers must catch more and more. As a result, the populations of the fishes that people want to eat have gone down. Because fishers can't find enough of those fishes to make a living, they hunt for others—such as sea horses—that they know they can sell. The number of fishers who depend on sea horses as a source of income has increased in recent years.

Not all sea horses are caught on purpose—some are caught by accident. Shrimp boats drag large nets across the sea bottom. The nets scoop up sea horses and other small fishes along with shrimps. Whether caught on purpose or by accident, the sea horses are sold. Trade, or the buying and selling, of sea horses occurs in more than 45 countries and territories.

Fishers drag nets like these along the ocean floor, catching many sea horses as well as other fishes.

Sea horses are traded for three main reasons. First, each year at least 20 million of them are used to make traditional medicines, especially in China. These medicines, which people buy to cure problems from feeling tired to liver and heart disease, can be purchased in countries all over the world.

Traders also buy and sell live sea horses for home aquarium use. Keeping sea horses as pets is popular in North America and Europe. Unfortunately, many aquarium owners don't understand that sea horses need lots of food and a balanced diet. They also get sick easily, and the diseases they get are hard to treat successfully. Most sea horses in home aquariums die rather quickly. Because sea horses don't breed easily in aquariums, replacements are captured from the wild.

Sea horses are also bought and sold to be used in decorative objects called curios. Key rings, paperweights, and pins made from dead, dried sea horses can be purchased in many countries. Hundreds of thousands of sea horse curios are sold each year.

Sea horses for sale in a Hong Kong pharmacy

This channel was dredged in Florida to create coastal land for houses. Dredging can uproot and destroy sea grass beds, leaving sea horses and other animals without homes.

Sea horse populations are threatened in another, less noticeable way. People often destroy sea horse habitats. When mangrove swamps are drained for coastline building projects, sea horses and many other animals lose their homes. Fishing nets that are dragged along the ocean floor uproot and destroy sea grass beds. Dredging, or the digging of channels, can also destroy sea grass beds. Some fishers use poisonous chemicals or dynamite, which can destroy coral reef communities. Mining companies dig out coral reefs and use the stone to make concrete. If sea horses and their habitats continue to be destroyed at the present rate, sea horses will become endangered.

What can be done to save sea horses? Banning the trade of sea horses is one idea. This solution would be hard to enforce, because so many people want to buy sea horses, and so many fishers need to sell them to survive. The sea horse trade would probably continue even if it were made illegal.

Villagers harvest fish at a small aquaculture center in the African nation of Burundi.

Aquaculture, or breeding sea animals in captivity for use in trade, has been attempted as a means of helping wild sea horses survive. On a large scale, however, aquaculture isn't practical. Providing enough food and preventing disease are very difficult. Although sea horses can breed in captivity, almost 90% of the young that are born die. Those that live and breed have small broods that again do not survive well. That means that the healthy adults needed to produce more young would still have to be caught and taken from the wild.

Suppose that a species such as *H. comes,*

which is in great demand for traditional medicines, became available through aquaculture. *H. comes* would be easier to buy, so it would cost less. That means that fishers would be paid less money for each *H. comes* caught in the wild. They would have to catch more *H. comes* to make as much money as they currently do, so more wild sea horses would die.

Although large-scale aquaculture isn't practical, small aquaculture centers located in fishing villages might help both sea horses and fishers. Fishers could sell the sea horses they raise, reducing the number they take from the wild.

Left: *Dr. Amanda Vincent* (left) *and Marivic Pajaro measure sea horses in a Filipino village.* Bottom: *Marivic Pajaro shows villagers how a male sea horse gives birth.*

Biologists and fishers have found other ways to help sea horses, other sea animals, and their habitats without ruining the fishers' livelihoods. Dr. Amanda Vincent and Marivic Pajaro, a Filipino biologist, worked with the people of Handumon, a village in the Philippines, to try to help the area's decreasing sea horse populations. The Handumon fishers depend on sea horses for as much as half of their yearly income, so they were concerned about the population drop. The fishers decided to keep the pregnant males they caught inside underwater cages until after the males had given birth. Once the baby sea horses had been born and released, the fathers were removed and sold.

The Handumon fishers also set up a **sanctuary,** a protected area where fish are not caught. The fishers agreed to patrol the area in boats to make sure fishers from other areas did not come into the sanctuary and catch fish.

So far, the sanctuary has produced encouraging results. The sea horse population has slowly increased, though not by a large number. The ban on fishing has allowed other fish populations—ones that fishers would prefer to catch—to grow and spread outside the sanctuary. Catching those fishes provides food for families and a few to sell. That means fishers don't need to catch as many sea horses.

Habitat protection is another benefit of these sanctuaries. Coral reefs, mangrove swamps, and sea grass beds gain time to grow, just as fishes do. And the healthier the habitats are, the healthier the whole network of plants, animals, and water will be.

Marine biologists and fishers from several southeast Asian and Pacific island villages hope to establish 50 more sanctuaries. If these sanctuaries develop like Handumon's, sea horse and other fish populations should benefit.

Handumon residents use this watchtower to guard their sanctuary.

Many questions about sea horses are still unanswered. Most sea horses species have never been studied in the wild. How long do sea horses live? How do they grow? Do they migrate, or travel? If so, where do they go? Do pair bonds remain faithful longer than a single breeding season?

As we learn more, we must continue to develop ways to protect sea horse populations while respecting fishers' needs. Solving the complicated problems of trade and habitat destruction will be a real challenge. The future of the world's sea horse populations will depend on how we meet that challenge.

GLOSSARY

aquaculture: the captive breeding and raising of fish and other water-dwelling animals for trade

breeding season: a specific time of year when a type of animal produces young

brighten: to change from a dull color to a brighter one

brood pouch: a sealed pocket, located on a male sea horse's tail, in which babies grow

camouflage: changing appearance to blend in with the surroundings

daily greetings: morning meetings between mated sea horses

embryos: animals that have not yet hatched or been born

endangered: at risk of dying out forever

feces: solid waste material produced by an animal

genes: tiny structures that determine the characteristics offspring inherit from their parents

habitat: the type of environment an animal or plant lives in

holdfast: an object that a sea horse wraps its tail around in order to anchor itself

home range: the area where an animal normally lives

larvae: animals that are in an early growth stage, after hatching

ovipositor: a tube that can extend outside a female sea horse's body to lay eggs

pointing: a courtship activity during which a sea horse raises its head and aims its snout upward

predators: animals that kill and eat other animals

prehensile: able to grasp objects

prey: animals that are eaten by other animals

pumping: a thrusting motion made by male sea horses during courtship and birthing

sanctuary: an area where animals are protected from being caught, harmed, or killed

species: a type of plant or animal

swim bladder: an air-filled organ that helps a fish rise or sink

tendrils: spiny skin growths that help a sea horse hide

trunk: the main part of a sea horse's body, excluding the head and tail

INDEX

ABOUT THE AUTHOR

From the moment that **Sally M. Walker** saw a television show about the unique characteristics and uncertain future of sea horses, she became determined to write a book about these amazing fish. Ms. Walker is the author of many books for children, including *Hippos, Rhinos,* and *Earthquakes,* all published by Carolrhoda Books. Although her favorite job is writing, she also works as a children's literature consultant and has taught children's literature at Northern Illinois University. While she writes, Ms. Walker is usually surrounded by her golden retriever and two cats, who don't say very much but provide good company. She lives in Illinois with her husband and two children.

The photographs in this book appear courtesy of: Visuals Unlimited: (© Ken Lucas) front cover, pp. 8 (top right), 30, (© Dave B. Fleetham) p. 8 (left), (© S. Maslowski) p. 8 (bottom right), (© A. Kerstitch) p. 23 (bottom), (© John D. Cunningham) p. 42; Tom Stack & Associates: (© Brian Parker) back cover, pp. 12 (top, middle), 16, 24, (© Ed Robinson) p. 10 (left), (© Mike Severns) p. 11 (top), (© Dave B. Fleetham) p. 20 (top), (© Denise Tackett) p. 21, (© Jack Stein Grove) p. 39, (© Tom Stack) p. 41; The National Audubon Society Collection/Photo Researchers: (© Dr. Paul A. Zahl) pp. 2, 9 (bottom right), 18, 29, 34, 36 (left), (© Gregory Ochocki) p. 9 (top right), (© Charles V. Angelo) p. 10 (right), (D. Roberts/Science Photo Library) p. 15 (top), (© Tom McHugh) pp. 15 (bottom), 28 (bottom), 35 (top), (© G. Soury/Jacana) p. 20 (bottom), (© Mike Neumann) p. 22, (© D. P. Wilson/David & Eric Hosking/Science Source) p. 23 (top), (© Fred Winner/Jacana) p. 28 (top); Peter Arnold, Inc.: (© Norbert Wu) pp. 4-5, (© Fred Bavendam) p. 11 (bottom), (© Secret Sea Visions) p. 19, (© IKAN (Kuiter)) pp. 25, 27, 36-37, 37 (right); © Bob Cranston, pp. 6, 17; *Equus marinis,* from the 1536 edition of Von Cube's *Orthus Sanitatis;* reproduced from "Olden Time Knowledge of Hippocampus," Charles R. Eastman, *The Smithsonian Report for 1915,* p. 7; © Norbert Wu, pp. 9 (left), 12 (bottom), 26; Animals Animals: (© R. Kuiter/Oxford Scientific Films) p. 31, (© Max Gibbs/Oxford Scientific Films) p. 45; King George V Memorial Hospital for Mothers and Babies, pp. 32, 33 (both); © Amanda Vincent, pp. 35 (bottom), 38, 40, 43 (both), 44. Map on p. 13 and illustration on p. 14 by Lejla Fazlic Omerovic, copyright © Carolrhoda Books, Inc.